ANCIENT CIVILIZATIONS

ANCIENT
MAYA

BY SUE BRADFORD EDWARDS

Essential Library

An Imprint of Abdo Publishing | www.abdopublishing.com

ANCIENT
MAYA

BY SUE BRADFORD EDWARDS

CONTENT CONSULTANT

Gerardo V. Aldana
Professor, Anthropology and Chicana and Chicano Studies
University of California, Santa Barbara

www.abdopublishing.com

Published by Abdo Publishing, a division of ABDO, PO Box 398166, Minneapolis, Minnesota 55439. Copyright © 2015 by Abdo Consulting Group, Inc. International copyrights reserved in all countries. No part of this book may be reproduced in any form without written permission from the publisher. Essential Library™ is a trademark and logo of Abdo Publishing.

Printed in the United States of America, North Mankato, Minnesota

102014
012015

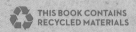
THIS BOOK CONTAINS
RECYCLED MATERIALS

Cover Photos: Oscar Espinosa/Shutterstock Images, foreground; Shutterstock Images, background

Interior Photos: Shutterstock Images, 2, 65, 89, 92; Jose Ignacio Soto/Shutterstock Images, 6–7, 62–63, 16–17; iStock/Thinkstock, 9; Serban Bogdan/Shutterstock Images, 9 (inset), 34; Don Wiechec/Bowers Museum/Corbis, 11; Frederick Catherwood/Gianni Dagli Orti/Corbis, 13; AP Images/Dario Lopez-Mills, 14; Fletcher & Baylis/Science Source, 19; Glow Images, 21; Peter E. Spier/National Geographic, 23; Richard A. Cooke/Corbis, 27; Galyna Andrushko/Shutterstock Images, 31; Jack Hollingsworth/Corbis/Glow Images, 32–33; Charles & Josette Lenars/Corbis, 36, 69; Oscar Espinosa/Shutterstock Images, 39; Ritterbach/F1online/Glow Images, 40–41; Werner Forman Archive/Glow Images, 43, 78–79; Enrique Perez Huerta/Demotix/Corbis, 46; Gianni Dagli Orti/Corbis, 49, 56; CM Dixon/Heritage Images/Glow Images, 50–51; De Agostini/Getty Images, 53; Wolfgang Kaehler/Corbis, 54–55; SuperStock/Glow Images, 60; Ingrid Deelen/Shutterstock Images, 70–71; Red Line Editorial, 73; Claus Lunau/Science Source, 76; Richard Schlecht/National Geographic Society/Corbis, 82, 84; Moises Castillo/AP Images, 86; Amanda Koster/Corbis, 95; Charles Rex Arbogast/AP Images, 96

Editor: Arnold Ringstad
Series Designer: Jake Nordby

Library of Congress Control Number: 2014943863

Cataloging-in-Publication Data

Edwards, Sue Bradford.
 Ancient Maya / Sue Bradford Edwards.
  p. cm. -- (Ancient civilizations)
ISBN 978-1-62403-540-1 (lib. bdg.)
Includes bibliographical references and index.
1. Maya--Juvenile literature. 2. Maya--History--Juvenile literature. 3. Maya--Social life and customs--Juvenile literature. 4. Indians of Mexico--Juvenile literature. I. Title.
972--dc23

                                                      2014943863

CONTENTS

CHAPTER 1

CITIES OF STONE

As King Chak Tok Ich'aak strained forward, the green feathers in his headdress caught the sunlight. Jade plugs stretched his earlobes. The crowd surrounding him and the other players roared. Their instructions and encouragement echoed off the stone temples and palaces surrounding the ball court in the city of Tikal.

The ruins of Maya ball courts can still be seen in Central America today.

Some people had come that day to trade in the great market, but the vast majority of visitors came to see an important match. Everyone, including Chak Tok Ich'aak, focused their attention on the ball that careened down the court. They shouted as it slammed into the stone floor outside the painted scoring zone.

Back in play, the ball hurled toward the other end of the court. A player from the opposing team intercepted it. He struck the solid rubber ball using the padded belt slung around his hips, and the force of the blow rocked him back on his heels.

Before it could strike the scoring zone, the captain from the other team dove beneath the ball, bouncing it off his upper thigh to a teammate. His belt and kneepads had protected him from serious injury, but every game was dangerous.

REDISCOVERING THE MAYA

By the time Christopher Columbus sailed to the New World in 1492, the stone cities of the Maya lowlands lay abandoned and overgrown by jungle. Some cities still flourished in the highlands. But in the lowlands, only the people who lived in nearby villages knew the cities were there. When outside explorers from the United States arrived in 1839, local guides were able to escort them to the ruins.

In that year, US President Martin Van Buren appointed John Stephens to be the nation's ambassador to Central America. Stephens did not get the job because of any diplomatic qualifications. Instead he got it for his experience in travel and exploration. He had heard about some of these Maya cities from other travelers.

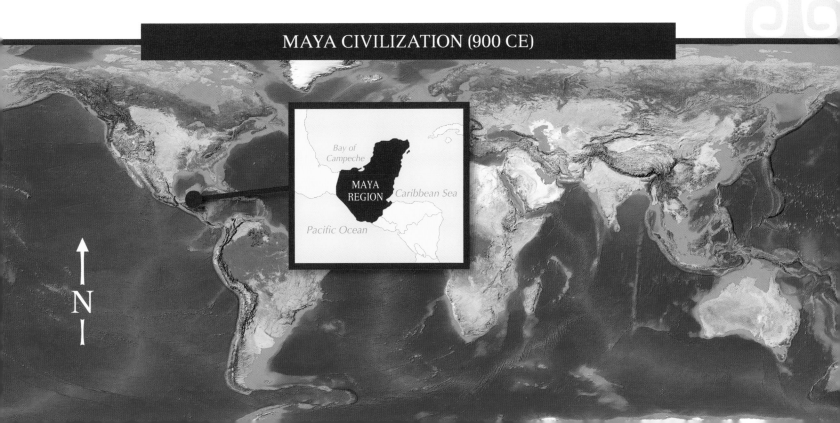

MAYA CIVILIZATION (900 CE)

Bay of Campeche

MAYA REGION

Caribbean Sea

Pacific Ocean

N

A CLOSER LOOK

DEPICTIONS OF BALLPLAYERS

The paintings on this vase show a ballplayer outfitted in the heavily padded belts players wore around their waists. Quilted cotton was wrapped around yokes made of wood. Some players also wore deer hides around these belts for even more cushioning. The Maya recorded images of ballplayers and their outfits on pottery and in stone monuments.

The players' garments provided protection from contact with not only each other but also the ball, a rubber sphere approximately 8 inches (20 cm) in diameter, just over twice as big as a softball.[2]

The game was played on a large court built in an I shape. Stone hoops were built into the walls. Platforms on the long sides provided seating areas for spectators. Players used their hips and buttocks to knock the ball into the hoop. The use of hands was not allowed.

The ball game was closely tied to Maya religion. One Maya creation story involves the game and a pair of twins. They find the ball equipment that belonged to their late father and begin to play, annoying the lords of the underworld by making too much noise. The lords of the underworld trick the twins into playing the game against them. However, the brothers win. They are able to resurrect their father, who is reborn as the maize god.

Stephens wanted to see the cities for himself, and this appointment gave him access to the countryside where the ancient Maya once lived. Their civilization had spread throughout Mexico's Yucatán Peninsula and the countries of Guatemala, Belize, El Salvador, and Honduras. Stephens took full advantage of this opportunity, exploring ruin after ruin.

Accompanied by painter Frederick Catherwood, Stephens explored a total of 44 ancient cities, including Copán, Palenque, Topoxte, and Tikal.[3] They began with sites other travelers had written about. Eventually they went on to explore ruins known only to local guides. The writing and artwork

Abandoned Cities

Studying ancient cities is dramatically different in other parts of the world. Exploring ancient Rome means digging beneath the modern city. Honking horns intermingle with the scrape of trowels. After the ancient civilization fell, people continued building in the same area. The situation was different in parts of the Americas. When the Maya left their cities, no one built over most of them. The forest reclaimed the land. John Stephens described the feel of these overgrown sites:

The city was desolate. No remnant of this race hangs round the ruins, with traditions handed down from father to son and from generation to generation. It lay before us like a shattered bark [ship] in the midst of the ocean, her mast gone, her name effaced, her crew perished and none to tell when she came, to whom she belonged, how long on her journey, or what caused her destruction.[4]

Catherwood's vivid artwork, published in popular books, provides stunning views of Maya ruins.

Stephens and Catherwood produced was published in two books that awakened new curiosity among the US public about these ancient cities and their builders.

ANCIENT BUILDERS

Stephens and Catherwood's books may have awakened an interest in the Maya, but many early visitors to these ancient cities misunderstood what they saw. They thought the Maya cities had been built by the Babylonians, the Phoenicians, or a lost tribe of Israel. Some artists even depicted Maya

hieroglyphs as including elephants, which did not exist in the Americas. They did not think the indigenous cultures of the New World were capable of producing such grand structures. They saw humble Maya villages and failed to understand how the same civilization could have built the impressive cities now in ruins.

For more than a century, archaeologists and other scientists have worked to piece together facts about the ancient Maya. The civilization's Classic period lasted between approximately 250 and 900 CE. At its peak in approximately 750 CE, it may have encompassed 13 million people.[5] The Maya used complex hieroglyphic writing systems to record much of what they did and discovered. Scholars are still working to decipher the words of the Maya as they uncover more and more of what these ancient people have to teach us about their stone cities.

Archaeologists continue to discover and explore Maya sites both above and below the ground.

What the Maya Said

Of the 28 modern Mayan languages spoken today, linguists have determined that Yucatec and Chol are most closely related to the language recorded in hieroglyphs.[6] Linguists have worked backward from these modern languages, studying what they have in common and how they are different. Identifying words that are similar in several languages can provide clues to the meanings of unknown words. And analyzing the grammar used by speakers of modern Mayan languages can help researchers piece together the grammatical rules of the earlier languages.

CHAPTER 2

FROM SIMPLE FARMERS TO CITY BUILDERS

From mountains and forests to the ocean and vast areas of wetland, the territory the ancient Maya called home provided a wealth of resources. This made it possible for them to build their great cities. However, the Maya were not the first people to take advantage of the lush region.

The lush Maya homeland has supported indigenous cultures for more than 10,000 years.

PALEO-INDIANS

The first people who lived in this area are known as the Paleo-Indians. They journeyed to the Americas from Asia approximately 14,000 years ago.[1] At that time, an ice age led to the appearance of a land bridge between the two continents. The Paleo-Indians walked across this bridge into North America, then traveled throughout Central and South America. Their tools can be found in Maya-occupied areas as early as 9500 BCE. There is also DNA evidence that people from Asia reached the Americas by boat across the Pacific.

The Paleo-Indians were hunter-gatherers who fed themselves by gathering wild plants and hunting various animals. Some groups followed the migrations of large animals. Others stayed in smaller areas, moving in seasonal paths to take advantage of the available plant and animal resources. Although they hunted large animals, including the now-extinct giant ground sloth, excavations in Mexico City show the Paleo-Indian people also hunted and ate small animals.

In approximately 8000 BCE, when the ice age ended and the climate warmed worldwide, many of the large animals of the Americas were unable

Evidence of the Paleo-Indian people includes footprints preserved in volcanic ash.

to adapt to the warmer, drier climate and became extinct. The people who lived in the Maya territories began domesticating plants and animals. Their diet continued shifting as they relied more on domestic food. Eventually they became settled farmers who lived in villages; wild food was only a supplemental source of nutrition.

Archaeologists have found evidence of the first permanent villages in the Maya region dating to approximately 1800 BCE. By 1000 BCE, villagers were making and using pottery. Archaeologists have identified these early potters as the ancestors of the Maya. Scientists do not know whether these Maya ancestors descended from the first farmers who lived in the area or if they moved into the region from elsewhere. However, they are certain that by 1000 BCE, the early Maya occupied the area where they would build a great civilization.

THE PERIODS OF MAYA CIVILIZATION

Scholars have divided the history of the Maya civilization into several distinct periods. The Preclassic period began with the first cities constructed in the Maya region. Some of the early cities are at the El Mirador and Kaminaljuyu sites. During the Preclassic period, the population increased dramatically, kingdoms became well established, and hieroglyphic writing was developed. This period ended by approximately 250 CE.

Palenque features some of the best-preserved Maya ruins.

The Classic period of the Maya lasted from approximately 250 to 900. Most of what people associate with the ancient Maya comes from the Classic period. Major cities from the era include Tikal, Palenque, and Copán. Trade, artistic production, and the writing of hieroglyphic texts peaked. The terminal phase of the Classic period lasted from approximately 900 to 1000. Many of the cities emptied out during this time.

The Postclassic period ran from approximately 1000 until contact with Europeans in the 1500s. Chichén Itzá, Uxmal, and Tulum are a few of the Postclassic cities in the northern Maya areas. The southern highlands of what is now Guatemala were home to the cities of K'iche' and Cakchiquel.

BUILDING UP

As the population in the area grew during the Preclassic period, the people spread to more villages. Villages grew to take advantage of stable trade routes. In these larger towns, people were divided into social classes. Wealthier citizens had a variety of luxury items, such as obsidian blades and exotic feathers, brought in by traders.

The massive stone cities of the Maya grew as some of these towns adopted a new type of leadership. Other cities throughout Mesoamerica had kings, but the Maya expanded on this idea. They established the high king. This king was more than just a man. He was a link to the gods.

The Maya believed their king acted as a pipeline between the Maya world and the supernatural world. Kings such as Tikal's Chak Tok Ich'aak linked people directly to their gods and funneled the tribute they received into a variety of building projects. These public works built up the great cities of the Maya civilization's Classic period.

CITY PLANS

Maya cities did not include streets and city blocks. Instead, they consisted of open plazas surrounded by a variety of buildings. At first, the groups of plazas may have looked haphazardly arranged. They were not organized along straight lines but instead followed the terrain, running along high, dry locations and leaving the fertile low ground open for farming.

Toward the center of the city stood the central plaza and the most important structures in the community: the government and religious buildings. These include the palaces where the king and lesser nobles lived, as well as enormous stepped pyramids topped with temples.

These temples were not built on natural hills but rather were constructed on man-made platforms. The platforms' internal walls held soil and other materials in place as weight was added to the upper levels. The pyramids were constructed with rubble cores and finished stone exteriors. Staircases climbed from the plaza up to the top of the temples.

As time passed, even these inner plazas and important buildings changed. Under the direction of the king, the people pulled down earlier

Dirty Details

Archaeologists work much like detectives. Their clues are found in tools and the other objects ancient people left behind. When there are no artifacts, they turn to specialists such as soil biogeochemist Richard Terry. Terry studies how chemicals are transferred between plants and animals and their environment. He examined the floors of Maya houses and plazas and found traces of phosphorus, an element that indicates food was prepared in the area.

At one time, archaeologists believed plazas were used for religious ceremonies. The phosphorus discovery provided evidence that these spaces were actually home to Maya markets. As in modern open-air markets, the Maya would sweep away debris at the end of the day. They would push leftover bits of food to the edges of the market. Terry did not find the food, but he did find a chemical fingerprint that helped archaeologists solve this Maya mystery.

temples and palaces when an important person died. They used the rubble to create mounds that would raise newer structures even higher. Over time, these layers of construction led to large pyramid buildings.

When the Maya sought out building materials, they looked as close to the building site as possible. They possessed only stone tools, and they had neither draft animals nor wheeled carts. Giant stone blocks had to be moved with nothing but human muscle. Archaeologists excavating in Tikal discovered the site where stone for the palaces and temples had been quarried. It later became part of the city's central reservoir.

They may not have been able to haul stone over great distances, but the Maya created buildings that reached several stories into the sky. Their construction included a unique kind of arch. The design, called a corbel arch, is sometimes known as a false arch because it lacks a keystone. The Maya arches used thick stone walls to hold up their weight.

Volcanoes?

The stepped pyramids of the Maya are impressive from the ground and from the air. Among the first pilots to fly over Guatemala's Mirador Basin was aviation pioneer Charles Lindbergh, who visited the region in the 1930s. When Lindbergh and his fellow pilots saw the vine-covered forms towering over the trees, they thought they were seeing volcanoes. In fact, the Maya built the pyramids as stand-ins for mountains, believing this would bring them closer to their gods and provide viewing areas for the development of their astronomy. The pilots had not spotted volcanoes crafted by nature, but rather mountains made by men.

A CLOSER LOOK

THE LABNÁ ARCH

This arch is located in Labná, in the southern Yucatán area. Although early visitors thought it was a gate joining two plazas, archaeologists now believe it was once a doorway to a building. The arch is an excellent example of the Maya corbel arch, with clearly visible stacked stones and without the keystone of a true arch. A corbel arch also lacks a true arch's smooth outline, looking much more like an upside down staircase. The walls into which these arches were built were thick to keep the weight of the arch itself from pushing the surrounding blocks outward and causing the wall to collapse.

Building several corbel arches in a row creates what is known as a corbel vault. The row of these vaults may have represented the layers of the Maya underworld. Use of the vault technique allowed the Maya to build roofs or second stories above the arches. Vaults typically measured approximately five feet (1.5 m) wide, though the largest reached 20 feet (6 m) in width. The steep roof made it easy to collect rainwater, a key advantage when other water sources were scarce.

The Maya began widely using the corbel arch in approximately 250 CE. A similar style of arch also saw use in ancient Babylon. Today, this method of arch building is infrequently used.

Stepping Up

The Maya believed mountains were the sacred dwelling places of their ancestors, reaching upward toward the gods. They also believed mountain caves were doorways into the underworld. In the Yucatán lowlands, no sacred mountains rose into the sky. The Maya solved this problem by building stepped pyramids. Both mountains and pyramids share the same name, *witz.* The Maya topped these steep-sided pyramids with temples that served as the burial places for the city's dead kings.

This led to a style of architecture based on straight lines, angles, and vast amounts of limestone.

Nestled among the stepped pyramids and palaces, near the central plaza, every city also had a ball court. This court had stone walls, often with plastered and painted stone floors. Ball courts in the northern Maya cities included stone rings set high on the walls for scoring opportunities.

From the ball courts to the immense pyramids and palaces, stone carvings of many kinds adorned Maya cities. These ranged from facades with elaborate decorative reliefs to staircases and masks on temple exteriors. The style of this artwork varied from city to city and across Maya time periods. Chichén Itzá is known for the immense, Classic-era serpents slithering across its buildings. Many of these carvings depict scenes from the lives of kings, including coronations and wartime victories. The vast majority of these carvings are found on stelae.

THE IMPORTANCE OF WATER

Maya craftsmen put considerable effort into their carvings, but a more mundane task took just as much of their attention. Ensuring a steady supply of water for their people was a top priority for Maya engineers.

The land on which the Maya built their cities and farms contained huge amounts of limestone. This soft rock is easy to cut, but it also erodes quickly. Rainwater remains on the surface for only a brief time before it passes through the stone and drips into caves and underground rivers. Local leaders had to make sure water was available in some other way.

In the northern regions, there are no rivers, and rainfall is the only source of water. When rain erodes the stone and the ground collapses, sinkholes known as cenotes open up. Inside these massive holes, the Maya built stairs. They climbed up and down to reach a steady supply of water even during the dry season.

The southern region is rich in rivers, which were important both for the water they provided and for trade purposes. Only when the population grew too large for the river to support them were the Maya forced to build reservoirs. The Maya had to capture rainwater before it drained away. They observed the landscape and noted where water collected. These were the places they chose to build their reservoirs.

The Maya Climate

Both in ancient times and today, rainfall in the Maya homeland has varied dramatically depending on the geography. Coastal regions may receive as little as 19.5 inches (50 cm) per year, while the mountainous areas may receive 157.5 inches (400 cm). Ninety percent of this rain falls during the wet season, which lasts from June until September.[3] Reservoirs helped to sustain the Maya cities during the dry season, between October and May.

When the people of Tikal quarried the stone they needed, they left behind an open canal that collected water from the central plaza. Water flowed through this canal into a reservoir in the middle of the city. To prevent the water from draining away, the Maya lined the area with stone slabs. They covered the stone with black clay they collected from nearby wetlands, forming a waterproof coating. The people then extended a wall around the reservoir so it could hold even more water. Tikal's system collected enough water to meet the needs of 10,000 people for approximately 18 months.[2]

Cities were often built around cenotes.

CHAPTER 3

CITY-STATES

When archaeologists write about the Maya and their cities, they are writing about a group of people who shared a common culture. The Maya spoke the same or similar languages, worshiped in the same way, and believed in the same religion. However, they did not identify themselves as a single group of people or live in one kingdom. No single king ever ruled all of the Maya lands.

Maya art often depicts the kings of individual city-states.

Maya cities were largely independent rather than being joined together into a single empire.

NOT ONE, BUT MANY

Instead of ruling over the Maya people as a whole, each king ruled over his own city and the surrounding villages and farms. Maya cities included Copán, Tikal, Naranjo, Calakmul, and Piedras Negras. Palenque was found in the mountains, and Uxmal, Mayapán, and Chichén Itzá were in the lowlands.

Maya kings formed an ever-changing network of alliances. Many of these agreements were made through marriage as one king married the daughter of a neighboring king or an important noble in another city. Alliances also formed when one king captured another in battle. Instead of sacrificing his captive, the victorious king would release the captured king to rule beneath him. Paintings on vases show one king paying another tribute items including fabric, feathers, and cacao beans. These beans were used for money and to make a chocolate drink consumed at banquets.

Despite these alliances, a united empire never developed among the Maya. This was in part because the victorious king did not absorb the land and people of the king he defeated. Victories and alliances were not used to gain territory but instead to win power. A king went to war for the prestige it brought him and the tribute items that would come into his city. At other times, kings aimed to solidify their dynasties or increase the flow of trade items into their cities. Archaeologists believe these priorities may have shifted in later periods. When Maya cities struggled to survive, they may have attempted to broaden their territories to increase their food supplies.

ROYALS

The right to rule a city passed from the king to his son. However, existing kings did not simply hand over the throne to their sons. Cities would thrive only when there was a strong king on the throne, so the new ruler had to prove himself in war before taking power.

If a king had no sons or if none of his sons were successful warriors, rule might be given to another male relative. Political reasons influenced the choice of heir. The hieroglyphic record suggests internal politics among the elite Maya were just as important as in modern power struggles. Only a strong ruler would succeed in taking and holding a Maya throne.

In recent years, scholars have found evidence that not all Maya rulers were male. Once, most experts believed royal women were mainly the wives or mothers of kings. But new research has revealed the existence of several Maya warrior queens. Maya artwork depicts them carrying shields or standing over prisoners of war. By analyzing inscriptions, Kathryn Reese-Taylor of the University of Calgary concluded that most of these warrior queens likely reigned after 623 CE.

FARMING

The different people of the Maya civilization had specific jobs to do. Maya kings busied themselves with rituals, politics, and economics. Scribes wrote about science, art, and important events in the kings' lives. Nobles advised the kings. Craftsmen used fine materials, such as obsidian, to create a variety of tools. Everyday people built their own objects from more common materials.

The milpa system of farming is still used by farmers in the modern Yucatán.

When Spanish settlers arrived in the Maya lands in the 1500s, they observed Maya farmers using a slash-and-burn system of farming. First, forests were cleared with fire. Then, fields known as *milpa* were set up and farmed for only two years before the soil was worn out.[1] Because this was the only type of farming directly observed by outsiders, archaeologists long believed the ancient Maya farmers used only this technique.

More recent finds show a wider range of agricultural methods, each designed to solve a particular problem. Archaeologists have found the remains of terraced fields. This allowed the Maya to grow crops on land that was otherwise too steep. The terraces kept rain from running rapidly downhill and eroding the soil.

Archaeologists also found evidence of raised fields. In areas that would be too wet to farm, the Maya dug canals that drained the water away. The fill from digging these canals was used to raise the fields. Farmers scooped soil and other material, including fish droppings, from the canals, dumping it onto the fields. This raised the fields further and also fertilized the soil. No matter where they grew their crops, one more challenge remained: moving the food from the fields into the Maya cities.

URBAN AGRICULTURE

When artists draw Maya cities, they show plazas surrounded by temples and palaces. Through recent finds, archaeologists know that beyond the central plazas, the smaller plazas often lay some distance apart, surrounded by individual homes and gardens.

Each of these smaller plazas was built on a small platform of limestone rock, boulders, and debris. In the center of these platforms stood houses that faced the small residential plaza. Particularly in dry areas, this plaza might include

Bones and Teeth

Archaeologists discovered that people in Copán farmed the hillsides from approximately 650 to 750 CE before returning to the old practice of only farming in the valley. These archaeologists also examined Copán skeletons and found porous bones and teeth with stress lines. These lines are not caused by chewing crunchy foods but rather by physical stress, such as poor nutrition. The skeletons of both peasants and nobles showed these signs of malnutrition, suggesting the diet of the later residents of Copán was less healthy than that of earlier people.

Raised stone platforms supported Maya buildings.

a cistern that collected and stored water. Eventually archaeologists realized these platforms and plazas had been built on elevated areas with poor soil. They found no signs of building in the richer soils, and they realized the surrounding areas had been farmed to produce food. This layout meant each city's food would be produced in or near the city itself. Large-scale crops, such as corn and cacao, were grown in high-concentration fields. However, household items such as spices and vegetables were often grown in small family gardens.

CHAPTER 4

MAYA SOCIETY

How a Maya man or woman lived depended greatly on what level he or she occupied in society. The most readily available information concerns the lives of the Maya elite. Surviving murals have taught archaeologists a great deal about the activity of kings and nobles.

Artwork has provided a great deal of information about Maya life.

Life in the Market

Maya art and writing often tell the history of kings or the movements of celestial bodies, but the murals at Calakmul tell about life in the marketplace. Glyphs describe the people in the paintings, including the "salt person" who carries a basket and spoon to scoop purchases out for customers, the "maize gruel person" who sells and ladles out corn, the "clay-vessel person" who sells pottery, and the "maize-bread person" who sells tamales.[1] These murals depict the bustle of the Maya marketplace.

The king lived a life of privilege, but he had many responsibilities organizing the lives of his people. Under the king were members of his family and other high-ranking nobles acting as merchants. They traded jade, obsidian, cacao beans, cloth, salt, and red spiny oyster shells for other goods the city wanted.

The king's farmers owed him a certain number of days of tribute labor each year; the king used these laborers to raise fields in swampy areas. Because fish lived among the water lilies in the canals that bordered these fields, their droppings fertilized the mud. Laborers hauled this mud into the fields, making the soil rich for crops, including cacao and cotton.

The king arranged all building projects, including temples, pyramids, and reservoirs. He acted as the organizing force that made the Maya city possible. For the Maya, his rituals ensured the gods would continue to favor them.

The nobles aided kings in many ways. An especially high-ranking noble might be sent to oversee a village allied with the king. The members of this ruling class were known as the *ajawtaak*. Individual rulers were called *ajaw*.[2] From among the nobility also came warriors, merchants, clergy, and scribes.

Archaeologists know both men and women were recognized as members of the nobility because they were both buried with elaborate paintings and wealthy grave goods, such as jade and pottery.

The Maya ruler K'inich Janaab' Pakal was buried wearing a jade mask.

Jade

Jade has been nicknamed Maya gold, a fitting description considering how highly the Maya valued this semiprecious stone. Jade's importance went beyond its physical beauty or its status as a treasure. Jade jewelry was the finery of choice for the maize god; the green of the jade symbolized the green growth of young cornstalks. Maya kings believed that like the maize god, they would battle and win against death and be reborn. They wore jade jewelry in preparation for this day.

The day-to-day activities of the nobility would vary according to how they served the king. A merchant might trek across the countryside to a foreign kingdom. A scribe might ink a book describing the passage of Venus through the sky.

Most Maya never traveled far from their homes unless they were merchants. There were only two ways to travel throughout the Maya lands: by canoe or by foot. Parties of merchants carried goods on wooden back racks, wearing wide-brimmed hats to shade their faces from the sun. What they carried varied depending on whether they were heading away from their home city or back again. Each city produced its own food, cloth, and basic ceramics but traded for other goods, such as basalt grinding stones, obsidian blades, and salt.

Beneath the king and nobles was a group of skilled craftsmen who created luxury goods, such as pottery, jade carvings, stone tools, shell jewelry, and beads. Archaeologists have found very little evidence of how these people spent their days. However, a few workshops have been identified by the waste materials left behind. Tiny stone flakes have been found in an obsidian workshop, and brine-boiling hearths were discovered where salt was made.

Peasant farmers were by far the single largest social group in Maya society. The days of both men and women were filled with work. When the call came for battle, farmers filled the ranks of the king's army. When great buildings were erected and roads were created, these men provided the sweat and muscle that moved the stones making up the Maya kingdoms.

DAILY DIET

At one point, archaeologists thought corn, squash, and beans formed the core of the ancient Maya diet. This had been the diet recorded by the Spanish in the 1500s. But a great deal of time had passed between the Classic Maya and the Maya encountered by the Spanish. Archaeologists now know that while corn was important to the Maya diet, there was also a great variety of foods available depending on where someone lived.

In addition to corn, which could be eaten as corn gruel or tamales, the Maya also cultivated a variety of trees. From these trees, they harvested cacao, palm fruits, avocado, and wild forest fruits such as the mammee apple, a reddish fruit with yellow flesh.

Maya who lived near the sea ate mollusks and saltwater fish. Inland Maya caught and ate freshwater fish. Archaeologists know some of the fish meat

The Maya used stone tools to grind cacao beans, corn, and other foods.

was salted to preserve it for later consumption. Maya also hunted deer, and there is some evidence they ate dog as well.

The evidence for their diet has not come from the remains of actual food; these items are uncommon because they decay quickly. Instead, evidence for the Maya diet has come from paintings on pottery. Chemical analysis of human skeletal remains can give additional insight into Maya nutrition.

FIRST IMPRESSIONS

For much the same reason archaeologists do not have Maya food to study, there is no ancient Maya clothing for them to examine. Instead they turn to artists' depictions painted on vases, inked in books, and carved in stone. These images show that clothing typically varied based on social class.

Most Maya artwork, whether it is paintings on pottery or engravings on jade, depicts the lives of the rich—kings, queens, and various nobles. The murals at Calakmul are one of the few depictions of everyday life in the Mayan world. These paintings show various workers preparing food, selling items, and serving customers in the marketplace.

The simplest clothing for men consisted of a loincloth and fabric headband worn across the forehead. Men of slightly higher status wore a fancier kilt instead of a simple loincloth, and their headdresses were also more elaborate. Even more ornate were the textiles, feathers, and jaguar skins worn by merchants. Women draped themselves in garments that looked like loose robes; some images show women in decorated blouses similar to the modern huipil. Both men and women wore wide-brimmed hats, most likely woven from plant fiber.

Kings, queens, and nobles dressed to impress everyone who saw them. This meant clothing was brightly colored and often decorated in creative patterns. Not surprisingly, the king wore the most elaborate clothing. During rituals and political functions he wore a towering headdress supported by a wooden frame that rested on his back. The headdresses combined patterned fabric and designs made from shell, jade beads, and feathers. The most desirable feathers for such a headdress were the iridescent green feathers of the quetzal. Sometimes the king's headdress would even include a mask of a god, such as the rain god Chac. The kings and the male nobles sometimes wore ceremonial costumes that looked like the padded belts of the ballplayers.

In addition to their clothing, Maya men and women wore a variety of jewelry. Both genders wore necklaces, including pectorals of jade that hung low on their chests. They also pierced their ears, sometimes wearing large jade plugs.

Maya elite modified their bodies in various ways. The skulls of infants were elongated by binding them between boards to create a flattened forehead and an oblong profile. Adults reshaped their teeth, filing them into points, notching the sides, or drilling the front surface to inlay them with a round jade bead.

The ornate clothing of the Maya kings made them easily distinguishable from the lower classes of the Maya social hierarchy.

Even in a crowded marketplace, no one would mistake a noble man or woman for a peasant farmer. Above them all towered the headdress of the king.

CHAPTER 5

WRITTEN WONDERS

When Stephens and Catherwood explored the Maya ruins in 1839, no one, not even their Maya guides, could read the hieroglyphs they found. Since then, a variety of scholars have looked for a way to decipher what these symbols have to say.

The ancient Maya left many examples of their writing behind, but only relatively recently have scholars been able to decipher it.

PICTURE PERFECT

When linguists look at a system of writing, they can tell a lot about it by the number of symbols it includes. A system with 20 to 35 symbols probably has an alphabet with each symbol representing a simple sound, such as *b* or *a*. A system with 80 to 100 symbols likely has a syllable-based alphabet with each symbol representing a consonant-vowel pair, such as *ba* or *di*. A system with a symbol for each word often has thousands of symbols.[1]

When linguist Yuri Valentinovich Knorosov examined the Mayan system in the 1950s, he discovered approximately 800 symbols. This was far too many for either type of alphabet, but not nearly enough for each symbol to represent a single word. Because of this, many scholars thought the Maya had a limited system with symbols for only a few hundred words.[2]

Knorosov knew written languages all use multiple types of symbols. He worked from notes written by Spanish bishop Diego de Landa, who

Glottal Stops

The spoken Mayan language includes a feature known as a glottal stop. This is the sound someone makes when they quit exhaling while talking. One example in English is the middle of "uh-oh." Glottal stops are most often written with an apostrophe mark as in the Maya word *k'ab*, which means hand. In this style, "uh-oh" would be written as "uh'oh." It may not seem like much, but taking away this brief pause can change one Mayan word into another with a completely different meaning. *K'ab*, meaning "hand," becomes *kab*, meaning "earth."[3]

Hundreds of years after he wrote them, de Landa's notes helped linguists decipher the Mayan alphabet.

lived in the Yucatán in the 1500s. De Landa had asked local scribes to record what he believed to be the Mayan alphabet, though he was unable to understand it himself. Hundreds of years later, Knorosov was able to use these notes to piece together the Mayan writing. Working with the hieroglyph for *west*, which combines two signs, he identified several consonant-vowel combinations.

A CLOSER LOOK

CARVINGS IN THE CITY OF COPÁN

In addition to carving freestanding statues, the Maya also carved figures on a variety of flat surfaces, including the frames surrounding doorways and stairs. Carvings like this one stood near temples and around various plazas. They commemorated events in the lives of Maya kings and queens. Carvings combined two Maya art forms, including both a portrait of the ruler and hieroglyphic writing that described whatever event was being commemorated.

Copán features some of the most impressive examples of these carvings. The site is located in what is now Honduras. This intricately carved gateway is located in Copán's east court, one of city's plazas. The location is well-known for its jaguar sculptures. Another key example of the carvings at Copán is the Hieroglyphic Stairway. Its dozens of steps feature more than 2,000 hieroglyphic symbols.[4]

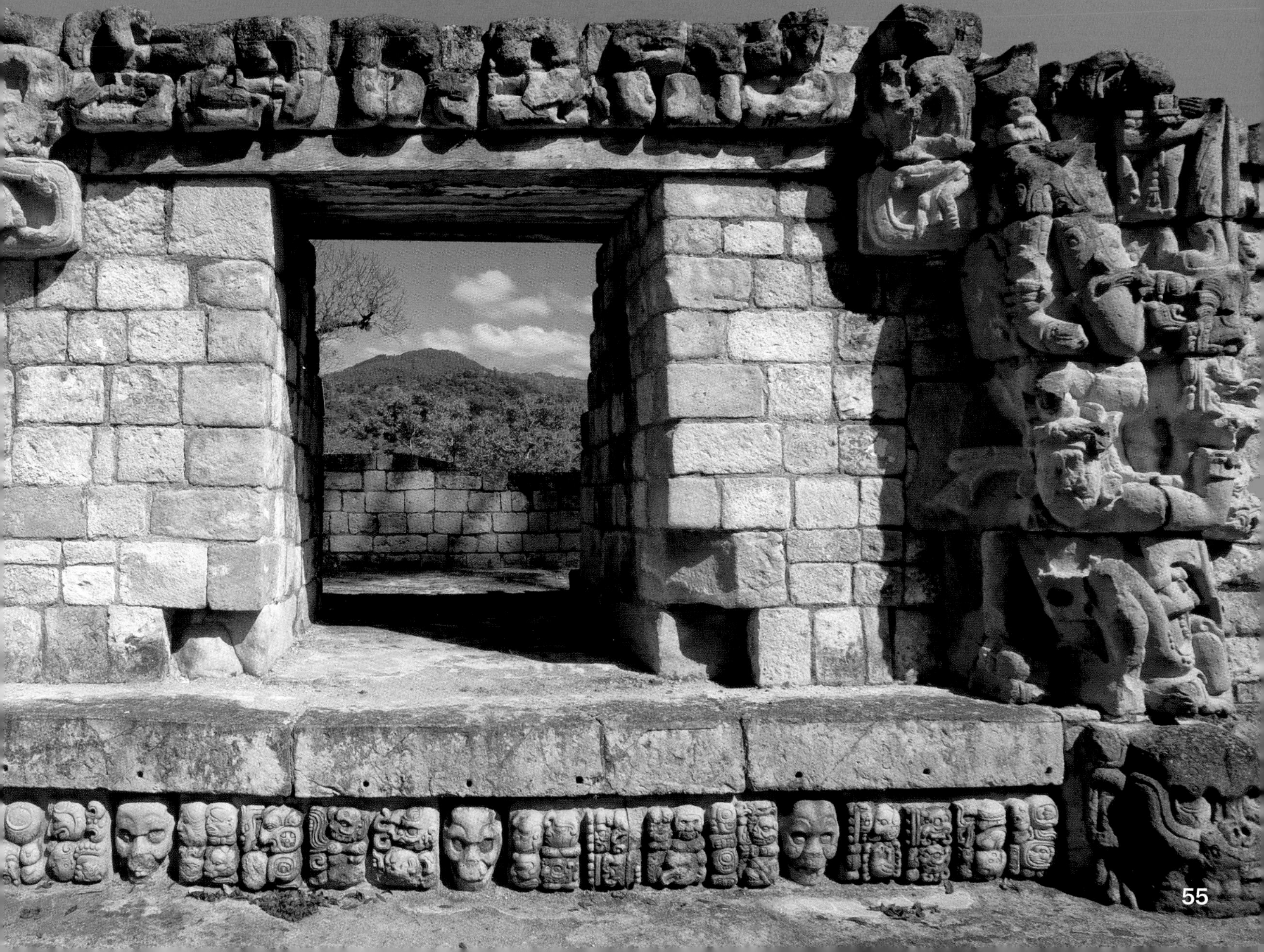

After Knorosov's work, archaeologists knew the Maya had a mixed system that used hieroglyphs for individual words as well as for syllables. Another breakthrough helped archaeologists understand what they were seeing in Maya art.

READING MAYA HISTORY

When archaeologists first discovered rows of stelae in front of Maya temples, they thought these stones recorded astronomical events or myths. Then, in the 1950s, Tatiana Proskouriakoff arranged photographs of stelae from the city of Piedras Negras in the order of their dedication dates, which archaeologists were able to read. Proskouriakoff was an artist hired by the University of Pennsylvania to illustrate the city's monuments. When she had the photographs in order by date, she spotted a repeating character within the inscriptions. In addition to the dates the stelae were dedicated, several stelae had another date accompanied by what she called the "toothache glyph." When she looked for additional patterns, she noticed another set of dates each accompanied by an "iguana head" glyph. The "iguana head" dates consistently fell 12 to 31 years before "toothache" dates.[5]

The stelae of Piedras Negras provided crucial clues to Maya history.

Proskouriakoff realized what she was looking at was not the story of Maya astronomy. She had uncovered the dynastic record of Piedras Negras' kings and queens. The iguana head glyph meant birth and marked the year a ruler was born. The toothache glyph marked the date he came to the throne. By combining the insights of Proskouriakoff and Knorosov, scientists were finally able to piece together a history of kings, battles, and thrones.

Epigraphy

Epigrapher David Stuart studies ancient Mayan inscriptions. His father was an archaeologist and took Stuart to various sites. Stuart drew the glyphs he saw. In 1984, when he was 18 years old, he was awarded a MacArthur Fellowship to study the glyphs further. He discovered each sound in the Mayan language was not represented by one symbol, but by as many as 15.[6] One symbol might be carved inside, overlapped, or joined with another.

SCRIBES

As richly complex as Maya society was, it was not a society of equals. At the bottom were the peasants and at the top were the nobility. Only those at the top learned to read. The scribes who served Maya courts came from this elite group.

The Maya writing system is challenging both to write and to read. This is in part because there is no one way to write a given word or phrase. The glyph for *sun* can be written in several ways, all of which have four spokes or petals.

Scientists have several different theories why there is so much variation. With no central Maya authority, Maya society as a whole was always fractured and fragmented. Alliances formed and dissolved, temporarily isolating cities from one another. Because of this, scribes may not always have had contact with each other. Each would have passed his or her knowledge on to only a small number of apprentices. In this way, each group of scribes would develop a distinct style.

Other Maya scholars believe the glyph a scribe decided to use at any given time was chosen using several criteria. These ranged from the artistic quality of the glyph to the practical matter of whether a particular glyph would fit in the space available. Like the scribes of medieval Europe who produced ornate manuscripts, Maya scholars used their artistic talents to generate elegant and pleasing combinations of glyphs.

Like artists today who paint, draw, and sculpt, scribes worked in a variety of different mediums. They carved limestone, telling of the deeds of their kings. They engraved jade, noting ancestral connections for the wearer. They recorded a wide variety of astronomical events in codices, folded books made of tree bark. They also painted the pottery that sealed alliances between Maya kings.

Codices Catastrophe

Evidence suggests codices were plentiful at the time of initial contact with Europe, but few now remain. In 1562, Spanish bishop Diego de Landa, who had the job of converting the Maya to Catholicism, burned many of these books. Other codices probably rotted in tombs. Between the moisture and the bishop, only four codices have been found for study.

Maya pottery came in a wide range of shapes, from plates for serving and eating, to vases for drinking cacao, to bowls for serving tamales. Archaeologists know exactly how some of this pottery was used because chemical analysis reveals the remains of the food. Other clues come from the paintings of feast scenes on the pottery itself as well as the hieroglyphs that tell who commissioned the piece, which scribe painted it, and how it would be used. Pottery, codices, stone carvings, and jade jewelry all contained the carefully crafted words of Maya scribes that reveal how the kings ruled and what courses the stars took through the sky. These writings give modern scholars insight into how the ancient Maya described the world around them.

Maya codices are filled with illustrations and glyphs.

CHAPTER 6

GODS AND SACRIFICES

The creation myth of one Maya city was recorded in the 1500s. It begins with water. It holds that long ago, water was all there was. The water contained six gods. Working together, these six deities created first the earth, then the sky, and finally the plants and the

The famous stepped pyramids of the Maya were an integral part of their religious beliefs.

63

animals. Only one problem remained. Because they could not speak, the animals could not worship the gods.

The gods decided to solve this problem by creating people. In their first attempt they made people out of mud. But these people lacked souls, so the gods sent a massive flood to destroy them. Next the gods fashioned people out of wood, but these wooden people still could not worship. When the gods destroyed them, some escaped and became the monkeys in the trees.

The gods tried one last time, making people out of a combination of white and yellow cornmeal. These people could speak, had souls, and correctly worshiped the gods. From corn, the gods created true, lasting humankind. The myth demonstrates the tremendous importance of corn to Maya society. The establishment of agriculture led to the high-density population of city life, so in that way corn actually facilitated their civilization's creation.

MANY LAYERS AND MANY GODS

The Maya believed the universe consisted of three layers. The lowest layer, beneath the world in which the Maya lived, was Xibalba, or the underworld. Much of this area was a deep, dark, disease-filled place. However, some parts were fertile or even comfortable. In these places, living kings and priests could enter the underworld to communicate with ancestors during religious ceremonies.

Ceiba trees are common in tropical areas around the world.

In the center of the universe was the world in which the Maya lived, a sacred place floating atop water. Some stories say it was on the back of a turtle, but others say the creature holding up the world was a caiman, a large reptile related to crocodiles and alligators. Growing up through the center of this world into the third layer, the sky, was the World Tree, or the Tree of Life. This was a ceiba, a type of tree common to the Maya lands. This tree connected the three worlds. Its roots reached down to Xibalba, its trunk stretched through the Maya world, and its branches grew into the heavens.

The Maya did not have one god but many. There was no clear hierarchy among them; for instance, during a hurricane, the god of storms might be more powerful than the god of the sun. Chac, the rain and lightning god, often appeared in artwork holding axes and snakes, which he used to affect the weather.

Some of the gods had more than one name and performed multiple functions. The Maya world was a complex place and it took a great deal of effort to keep so many gods happy and working together for the good of the Maya. It was the job of the priests and the king to decipher the heavens and make sure all was well for the Maya.

CARDINAL DIRECTIONS

The world the Maya lived in was divided not only into layers but also into the four cardinal directions. At the center of these four compass points was the center of all things, the World Tree. As in many other cultures, the

Maya associated each direction with a color; the color of the center was blue-green. Maya kings symbolized this center.

Of the four directions, east was the most important because it was the direction in which the sun rose. The Maya believed each morning the sun was resurrected after making a nightly journey through the underworld, the land of death. Because of this association between the east and rebirth, the Maya buried important people on the eastern sides of plazas and patios. The color for the east is *chac*, or red.

The Maya thought of the south as the left-hand side of the sun. The color of the south was *kan*, or yellow. The west, associated with the death of the sun each night, was assigned *ek*, or black. The north, also known as the side of heaven, was the direction from which the rains came. Its color was *zac*, or white.

BLOOD

The Maya believed the gods were the source of all life. They had created the world, the animals, the plants, and even people. These same forces of nature, including the sun and rain, continued to keep the world alive. They expected something life-giving from mankind in return.

Central to some rituals practiced by the Maya was a form of sacrifice called bloodletting, a practice the Maya believed activated the soul and connected the Maya with the living force of the entire universe. A Maya noblewoman who wanted to speak to an ancestor would first pierce her tongue with a stingray spine and then pass a cord with thorns embedded in it through the wound, causing even more blood to flow. She collected her blood on strips of paper that she would then burn. As the smoke from this blood sacrifice curled upward, she would be able to look into it and see both the gods and her beloved ancestors.

The Maya collected blood offerings in a variety of ways, including running the thorn-embedded cord over a cheek or lower lip. Cuts were also made with obsidian blades. Archaeologists know bloodletting was not limited to only the kings and queens, because the obsidian blades have been found throughout Maya villages. Some blades were simply used as knives in everyday household use, but they also made it possible to practice bloodletting in private rituals.

Blood was considered a worthy and essential payment for the gods to continue favoring the Maya with the daily sunrise and the movement of the moon and the stars. The most powerful blood of all was that of a king, a man who could speak to the gods.

Jade chest ornaments known as pectorals feature images of ancestors and were often buried with elite members of Maya society.

CHAPTER 7

MATHEMATICAL MARVELS

Astronomy and the calendar played an enormous part in the lives of the ancient Maya, but this was possible only because of their understanding of mathematics. Their understanding of numbers was so advanced they were one of only three cultures worldwide to independently develop the concept of

A building known as El Caracol, located at Chichén Itzá, may have been used as an observatory.

zero. The Maya gave it a symbol within their writing system and worked with it in making calculations.

ZERO THROUGH TWENTY

The Maya system of mathematics differed from the decimal system, or base ten, that is utilized almost universally today. In the decimal system, each place represents a value of ten, starting with ones on the far right, then moving left to tens, then hundreds, and so on.

Maya numerals were written vertically using dots, bars, and a symbol, such as a shell, for zero. The numbers 1 through 19 were written using dots and bars. A dot represented 1 and a horizontal bar represented 5. For instance, the number 3 would be three dots side by side. The number 8 would be a horizontal bar with three dots over it. And the number 17 would be three bars with two dots over it.

Rather than using four bars for 20, a shell was placed where the dots and bars would be. A dot was placed above it. This indicated a 1 in the twenties place and a 0 in the ones place. Today, scholars represent this as 1.0. The number 21 would be written with a dot in the twenties place and a dot in the ones place, and today it would be written as 1.1. The number 62 would be written as 3.2.

MAYA NUMBERS

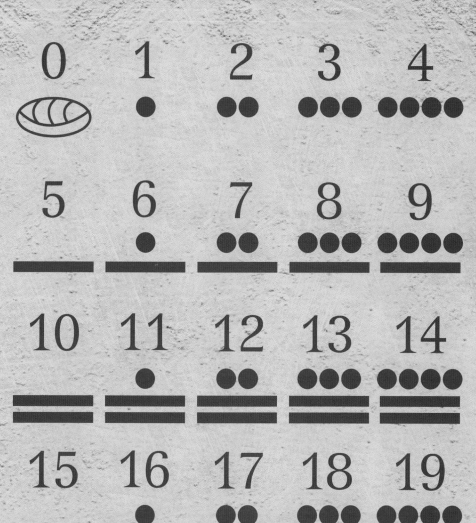

Viewing Venus

When the Maya built observatories such as El Caracol in Chichén Itzá, they designed the building so each element lined up with an astronomical event. In El Caracol, the lower platform faces the northernmost point where Venus sets, which happens once every eight years.[1] Lines of sight run from the corners of doors and windows to the northernmost and southernmost points at which Venus rises and sets. Lines of sight also extend toward the position of the sun on the two annual equinoxes, the dates when night and day are of equal length.

The Maya used this base-20 system to maintain a complicated system of calendars and predict astronomical events, such as eclipses and the position of the planet Venus.

NOW YOU SEE IT

Astronomy played a central role in many aspects of Maya life because of Maya beliefs about the universe and their place in it. Not only did the Maya exist between the underworld and the heavens, but they also believed they stood at the center of the universe. The Maya carefully observed the sun, moon, stars, and planets. They did so not only because they believed these bodies were gods and goddesses, but also because they believed the objects influenced human lives. As a result, Maya kings and queens planned many aspects of their lives and those of their people around the motion of the sun, the moon, and the stars.

The Maya drew on their calendar system and various mathematical calculations to predict eclipses, equinoxes, and the zenith position of the sun as well as the general paths of the moon, planets, and stars. The movements of these bodies created a complex system through which the Maya regulated their lives. As they tracked these dates and listed when various events would repeatedly occur, the Maya looked for cycles far into the future.

CALENDAR COUNT

The Maya system of calendars consisted of four interrelated calendars: the tzolkin calendar, the haab calendar, the calendar round, and the Long Count.

The tzolkin calendar, also known as the Sacred Calendar, was used to determine lucky dates for various activities. It used 20 day signs and 13 numbers to create a cycle of 260 days. A tzolkin date would be written as 4 Ajaw, the number followed by the day sign.

The haab calendar, also known as the Vague or Solar Calendar, was used by farmers to coordinate the planting and harvesting of their crops. It used 18 month names, each month having 20 numbered days. An additional five unlucky days per year brought the

The Three Hearthstones

Different cultures trace different patterns of stars in the night sky to create constellations that are meaningful to them. When the Maya gazed up into the night sky and glittering stars, they did not see the constellation Orion known to the ancient people of Europe. The Maya called the three bright stars of Orion the Three Hearthstones. The triangular arrangement of stars reflected the importance of the hearth as the center of the Maya home.

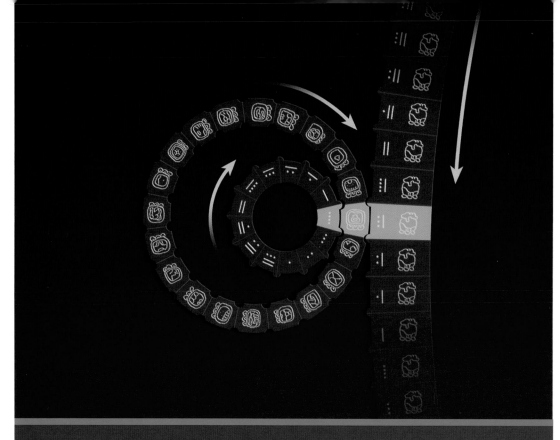

The tzolkin calendar can be visualized as three connected wheels. The smallest shows the 13 numbers, the next largest shows the 20 day signs, and the biggest is the complete cycle of 260 days.

count to a total of 365 days. Like the tzolkin calendar, dates were written as the number of the day followed by the name of the month. For instance, 8 Cumku would be the eighth day of the month Cumku.

The tzolkin and haab calendars had been invented by the neighboring Olmec people, but the Maya used a merger of the two calendars called the calendar round. Since the least common multiple of 260 and 365 is 18,980, that was the length of one calendar round year. Any single date will not repeat for 18,980 days. A date in the calendar round is given by stating both the tzolkin and haab dates, such as 4 Ahua 8 Cumku.

The Maya Long Count calendar provided a way to fix a date in time. It started with a zero date in the distant past, and then it counted forward from this set point in time. Much of the calendar was designed around the Maya base-20 counting system. Celebrations were held at the completion of 20-year periods and 400-year periods.

The Maya saw their world as a complex place, and they relied on their knowledge of astronomy and the workings of their calendar system to determine their place in it and how they might make this work to their advantage.

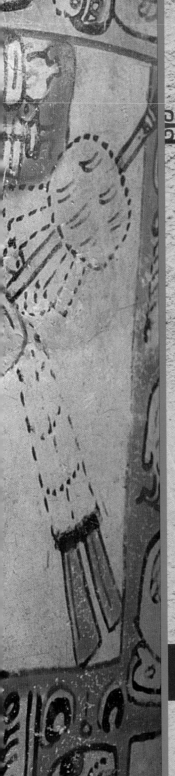

CHAPTER 8

AT WAR

Before the Maya language was deciphered, few who studied the Maya talked about their military or wars. Scholars believed these kings, astronomers, and deep thinkers did not belong to a culture of war. This view of the Maya changed once scholars discovered murals that show Maya warfare.

Images of Maya warriors have shed light on the military history of the ancient Maya.

Limited Manpower

Because the Maya had no draft animals, such as horses, oxen, camels, or llamas, every item that moved through their lands had to be moved on the back of a human porter. Men with back racks carried trade items to the market and tribute items to the regional king.

Porters also carried supplies for Maya armies. The distance they could travel was limited, however. Human porters could carry much less than the horses used in Europe. They also needed to consume some of their own supplies to keep up their strength. The greater the distance they carried the corn, the more they had to eat, leaving less for the warriors.

NO ONE ARMY

Just as there was no one king over all the Maya territories, there was not a single army. Every king had his own army made up of men from his city and the surrounding countryside. They were truly his army, not just because they fought to defend his city, but because he fought alongside them. Kings and even ruling queens led their own armies because military victories and taking captives were the way for a Maya leader to win the respect of the people.

While the armies of ancient Rome and ancient China could easily number into the tens of thousands, a force of several thousand was an immense army by Maya standards. Maya elite most likely acted as officers, helping the king guide his forces in battle, but the bulk of the fighters were peasant farmers.

STONE AND STICKS

Unlike other ancient fighting forces, Maya warriors did not fight in gleaming armor or carry masterfully crafted swords. Their equipment was limited by the level of technology they had available. Because they had no metals, they lacked weapons such as swords, pikes, and maces that are often associated with ancient warfare. This also meant they had no metal armor. Some experts believe that in the Postclassic period, they might have used quilted body armor. But during the Classic period, warriors carried no more than small shields.

Long-range weapons including slings, javelins, and atlatls have been seen in painted images. However, Maya battles consisted mostly of close quarters, hand-to-hand fighting using spears.

SNEAKY SKIRMISHES

When Maya armies clashed, they seldom met in open battle for a pitched, prolonged fight. Instead they specialized in small, frequent raids with one force sneaking up on another or perhaps even stealthily entering a city. The skirmishes may have been small and brief, but they were also frequent.

Sometimes walls were built within individual Maya cities or even along a border. One example is the wall protecting the northern border of Yaxchilan. Such walls were erected to limit where the enemy could pass between two

hills, funneling them into a restricted area and making them more vulnerable. For many years, these walls went unnoticed by archaeologists. Eventually, scholars hired local Guatemalan guides who had fought in Guatemala's civil war during the 1980s and 1990s. These men helped the archaeologists see how the terrain might have been used to aid in defense. Following this new understanding, more defensive walls have been identified.

CAPTURE

Before becoming king, a would-be heir sometimes took captives in battle. This increased his standing among his people and with neighboring cities. A king from a bordering city would be less likely to attack another king if he expected strong resistance. To get the message across even to those who could not read, sculptures of successful kings and queens often show them standing on top of their captives.

The Dry Season

Maya kings largely limited their warfare to the dry season. There were two important reasons for this. First, the men that made up the backbone of their armies were also the farmers the kings relied upon to feed their people. Farmers could not put off planting, caring for the fields, or harvesting. However, they could put off fighting until the dry season when there was relatively little to do. Keeping warfare to the dry season also prevented having to travel during the heaviest rains of the year.

Aguateca, a Maya city with defensive fortifications, was the site of a major battle in approximately 810 CE. Its ruins are key resources for learning about Maya warfare.

Maya cities used artificial walls and natural features of the landscape to protect themselves.

As the Maya population grew, defensive walls went up around border cities. Sometimes the surrounding population actually moved to live within the walls. Fighting over resources may have sparked more warfare as the Maya civilization began declining.

As scholars translate more Mayan writing, they learn more about Maya warfare. However, it is not easy to decipher the details of Maya warfare because the facts are not all in one location. As Zach Zorich, editor of *Archaeology* magazine, notes, "Among the Maya, the victors literally did write the history. Rulers were proud to commemorate their successful military campaigns, while the losers typically did not record their defeats."[1] This means that to get a complete picture of what was going on between two rival kings, archaeologists must study the monuments in both cities. Little by little, they are piecing together the complex history of the Maya.

CHAPTER 9

HERE AND GONE

W hat happened to the Maya, and where did they go? Archaeologists know the answer to the latter question. The descendants of the Maya still live in Central America today. But experts are still debating what brought about the Maya civilization's downfall.

The modern Maya people still incorporate their ancestors' ceremonies into their lives.

CAUSES OF COLLAPSE

When archaeologists talk about the fall of the Maya, they discuss a variety of causes. Population growth may have outpaced the supply of natural resources. Overfarming and deforestation could have degraded the environment through erosion. Increased warfare may have torn apart societies. Or perhaps changes in the climate, such as droughts, made it difficult for the Maya to survive. All these factors may have played a part. The two with the most compelling evidence are deforestation and drought.

The region had been supporting immense populations for a long period of time. People in cities and towns used wood to fuel their cooking fires. Most of what they cooked was grown on lands once covered by forests. Trees also fueled the fires that cooked the lime plaster covering the Maya's stone buildings. Researchers estimate it took approximately 20 trees to prepare the plaster needed to build 11 square feet (1 sq m) of Maya cityscape.[1]

Deforested land contributes to drought as well. Land cleared of trees absorbs less heat from the sun than land that is still forested. Less heat absorption leads to less evaporation, which in turn reduces clouds and rainfall. Simulations estimate this process reduced rainfall in the Yucatán

Some archaeologists believe drought caused the collapse that left Maya cities and ball courts empty and deserted.

Tikal National Park

The World Heritage List, compiled by the United Nations World Heritage Center, features 981 sites that contain globally important natural or cultural resources. Tikal National Park is one of only 31 sites that fit into both categories.

Visitors can see remains of more than 3,000 ancient Maya buildings, as well as 2,000 plant species, 54 mammal species, 333 bird species, and 38 snake species.[4] Among these plants and animals are endangered species, including the jaguar.

at the time of the Maya collapse by as much as 15 percent.[2]

Archaeologist Richardson B. Gill supports the idea that drought led to the collapse of Maya cities. He discovered the driest period in 7,000 years took place between 800 and 1000 CE, a time period that coincides with the collapse of the Classic Maya.[3] In 799, Palenque's last king took the throne. A stela from the last king of Naranjo was erected in 820. The final stela inscribed with a long count date in El Caracol was erected in 859, and the final one in Tikal was erected in 869.

Some archaeologists disagree with Gill's conclusion, pointing out that the entire Maya region did not collapse at the same time. They note the wetter southern region actually collapsed before the drier northern region. However, Gill's supporters argue the reason why the south collapsed was because of the landscape the Maya occupied.

In the south, people depended on their reservoirs and cisterns. Although the Maya in these areas could store water, they could only do so if it rained. A long dry spell would not only deplete their stores, it would also mean these same stores would not be replenished. Overall, the south may have been wetter, but even a short drought is cataclysmic if rainfall is a city's only source of water. In the drier north, the Maya lived at a lower elevation. This meant they could either dig wells or reach the aquifer through a cenote.

Eventually, even the north suffered from the drought. In approximately 400 CE, the first people to live in Chichén Itzá built the earliest part of the city around a cenote. By approximately 987 CE, a second well came into use. Substantial rains did not come, and the city was gradually deserted.

THE COLLAPSE

The reality is that when archaeologists and historians speak of the Maya collapse, they refer to the system of kings, nobles, and cities rather than the Maya people. The Maya still traded with each other, but they traded for goods such as salt and stone tools rather than the luxury items desired by their kings and the nobles. They still worshiped their gods, but they did so in rituals focusing on family and home instead of in ball games and religious ceremonies in crowded plazas. The cities did not empty out immediately.

Archaeologists discovered that in the city of Yaxchilan people built their homes in plazas no longer used for official functions. They used rubble from broken monuments as part of their foundations.

When the last king of Copán fell, the people did not abandon the city. They continued living in the residential plazas not far from the main plaza and its mighty buildings. It was not until a building collapsed that people completely abandoned the once mighty city.

LEARNING FROM THE MAYA

It is not surprising that people today are still studying the Maya. There are still Maya mysteries to solve, but that is not all the Maya have to offer. Scholars are studying the Maya to see what these ancient city builders might have to teach us about some of the problems facing modern cities.

Maya Apocalypse

The Maya came to international attention in 2012. On December 12 of that year, the Maya Long Count calendar shifted to a new period. However, a few people believed the cycle's end meant the world would come to an end. To Maya experts, this was a bizarre belief. The Maya calendar did not end on this date; it simply moved to the next cycle, just as today's common calendars move on to a new century. Still, the idea of a cataclysmic event occurring on December 12, 2012, gripped the public's imagination. A big-budget Hollywood movie, titled *2012*, even included such an event in its plot.

Traditional Maya homes were built from fast-decaying materials such as wood and mud, meaning they were frequently built and rebuilt.

Archaeologist Michael E. Smith of Arizona State University says, "Archaeology furnishes a record of urban success and failure over thousands of years in many parts of the world. Why did some flourish for centuries while others grew and declined over a decade or two?"[5] City planners today are working to solve problems related to the spread of urban development, an issue the Maya also faced.

One thing planners are studying is the inclusion of green space within cities. These green areas included small-scale agriculture that led archaeologists to call these Maya centers green cities, garden cities, and forest gardens.

By learning how the Maya fed tens of thousands of people in cities without complex technology, today's scientists may gain insight into current social problems, such as providing affordable food for an ever-growing urban population. The Classic Maya sustained their civilization for almost 700 years, demonstrating the effectiveness of their practices.

MAYA TODAY

Today, several million people of Maya descent still live within traditional Maya lands. As the Spanish conquered the region, many Maya people were forced to accept Catholicism. Others chose to maintain their own traditions and moved away from European settlers. Scribes who wrote the Mayan

Descendants of the ancient Maya still farm their lands today.

language were executed, and codices were burned. Despite this, modern Maya still speak Mayan languages. Many of their customs, from farming and clothing to some religious ceremonies, are similar to those of their ancestors.

The use of traditional weaving techniques is one of the ways in which modern Maya people stay connected to their shared past.

Modern Maya women still weave, making traditional blouses called huipiles. A huipil is made from a rectangular piece of cloth woven flat, then removed from the loom so the sides can be stitched together. In a Maya myth, the goddess of the moon taught women how to weave.

Each weaver has her own design for the decorative patterns, but these designs often contain images found in ancient art. One of these elements is the diamond shape that represents the universe. It can be found on huipiles from villages in the Mexican state of Chiapas.

The Maya in Belize and Mexico are among those nations' poorest citizens. Yet they are using the political systems within their respective countries to speak out and improve their lives. The Maya people living in these areas today do not focus their attention on the past glories of the ancient Maya. Instead their focus is on shaping politics and environmental policies to improve the standing of both themselves and their ancestral lands. The Maya have not disappeared.

Blending Two Faiths

The Maya today frequently blend aspects of Catholicism and the ancient Maya religion. "Modern Maya see little conflict in merging the two faiths," says anthropologist Robert M. Laughlin.[6] Laughlin has lived among the Maya for more than 30 years. "It is common on feast days for a procession to begin at the Church of San Lorenzo with a mass for Christ the Sun God and his mother the Moon Goddess, and then proceed to a nearby hill for the veneration of ancestors and Maya gods."[7]

TIMELINE

9500 BCE
Paleo-Indian people arrive
in Central America.

1800 BCE
The first permanent villages in the
Maya region are established.

1000 BCE
The earliest discovered Maya
pottery is created.

C. 250 CE
The Maya civilization's
Classic period begins.

360–378
Chak Tok Ich'aak rules in Tikal.

400
The first buildings in Chichén Itzá
are built around a cenote.

799
Palenque's last king takes the throne.
Shortly after this, the site is abandoned.

800–1000
The driest period in 7,000 years occurs.

820
A stela of the last king of
Naranjo is erected.

859
The last stela with a Long Count
date in El Caracol is dedicated.

869
The last stela with a Long Count date in Tikal is dedicated.

C. 900
The Classic period ends.

1500s
The creation stories of the Popol Vuh are recorded by Maya people in Quiché, Guatemala.

1500s
The Spanish arrive and conquer the Maya towns in northern Yucatán and highland Guatemala.

1562
Bishop Diego de Landa burns Maya codices.

1839
John Stephens and Frederick Catherwood explore Maya ruins.

1950s
Yuri Valentinovich Knorosov and Tatiana Proskouriakoff make important breakthroughs in the study of Mayan glyphs.

1984
Epigrapher David Stuart is awarded a grant to study Mayan glyphs.

2012
On December 12, a period of the Maya Long Count calendar ends.

ANCIENT HISTORY

KEY DATES

- **1000 BCE:** The earliest known Maya artifacts were created.

- **300–900 CE:** The Maya civilization underwent its Classic period, making advances in technology, mathematics, and culture.

- **800–1000:** A dry period may have contributed to the civilization's downfall.

- **1500s:** The Maya make first contact with European people.

KEY TOOLS AND TECHNOLOGIES

- Technologies related to farming and water conservation made it possible for the Maya to settle in centralized cities, grow, and thrive. Reservoirs allowed cities to store water for use during dry periods.

- The Maya recorded information in codices using their complex written script.

- An advanced understanding of mathematics let the Maya make accurate calendars of astronomical predictions.

LANGUAGE

The ancient Maya used a hieroglyphic writing system. Several different Mayan oral languages were spoken in the ancient Maya world. Descendants of many of these languages are still spoken today.

MAYA CALENDARS

- The tzolkin calendar has a cycle of 260 days and was used for religious purposes.

- The haab calendar has a cycle of 365 days and was used for agriculture.

- The calendar round combines the Tzolkin and Haab calendars and has a cycle of 52 years.

- The Long Count calendar began at a zero date in the distant past and was used to fix dates in time.

IMPACT OF THE MAYA CIVILIZATION

- The exploration of Maya lands led to advances in archaeology and linguistics. Learning how to decipher the written Maya language has enabled experts to piece together the history of a once-great civilization.

- Maya methods of growing and transporting crops still inspire people to develop more efficient ways to farm in and around cities.

- Goods such as rubber and chocolate come from the Maya region and have been important since the colonial period.

QUOTE

"The city was desolate. No remnant of this race hangs round the ruins, with traditions handed down from father to son and from generation to generation. It lay before us like a shattered bark [ship] in the midst of the ocean, her mast gone, her name effaced, her crew perished and none to tell whence she came, to whom she belonged, how long on her journey, or what caused her destruction."

—*explorer John Stephens*

GLOSSARY

aquifer
An underground water source.

archaeologist
A scientist who learns about a group of people by studying what they
left behind including buildings, artifacts, burials, and trash.

atlatl
A device that allows the user to throw a spear.

calendar round
A calendar that combines the haab and tzolkin calendars to create a cycle of 18,980 days.

cenote
A sinkhole.

cistern
An underground tank or reservoir for storing water.

epigrapher
Someone who studies ancient inscriptions, such as Mayan or Egyptian hieroglyphs.

glyph
A symbol based on a picture.

haab
The 365-day solar calendar used by Maya farmers to properly
time the planting and harvesting of their crops.

huipil
A traditional fabric garment of Mexico and Central America typically made using a backstrap loom.

jade
A green stone often used to make jewelry and other goods.

keystone
A wedge-shaped stone located at the top center of a traditional arch that helps lock the other stones into position and support the arch structure.

linguist
A person who studies languages and how they function.

reservoir
The body of water that supplies a community.

stela
An upright stone slab used to commemorate significant dates in the reign of a king or queen.

tribute
A payment from a city-state to a more powerful nation.

tzolkin
A Maya calendar used to set the dates for various religious rites.

zenith
The point in time at which something reaches the height of its power.

ADDITIONAL RESOURCES

SELECTED BIBLIOGRAPHY

Coe, Michael D. *Breaking the Maya Code.* London: Thames, 2012. Print.

Martin, Simon. *Chronicle of the Maya Kings and Queens.* New York: Thames, 2000. Print.

Sharer, Robert. *The Ancient Maya.* Stanford, CA: Stanford UP, 2006. Print.

FURTHER READINGS

Buckley, A. M. *Mexico.* Minneapolis, MN: Abdo, 2011. Print.

George, Charles. *Maya Civilization.* Detroit: Lucent, 2010. Print.

Somervill, Barbara A. *Ancient Maya.* New York: Children's Press, 2013. Print.

WEBSITES

To learn more about Ancient Civilizations, visit **booklinks.abdopublishing.com**. These links are routinely monitored and updated to provide the most current information available.

PLACES TO VISIT

THE METROPOLITAN MUSEUM OF ART

1000 Fifth Avenue

New York, New York 10028

212-535-7710

http://www.metmuseum.org

The Metropolitan Museum of Art in New York City features many Maya artifacts, including vessels, plates, and figures.

TIKAL NATIONAL PARK

1-800-297-1880

http://www.tikalpark.com

This site is a Guatemalan national park and a United Nations–designated World Heritage site. Tikal National Park in Guatemala features Maya ruins and native wildlife.

SOURCE NOTES

Chapter 1. Cities of Stone

1. Simon Martin. *Chronicle of the Maya Kings and Queens*. New York: Thames, 2000. Print. 28.

2. Michael D. Coe. "Another Look at the Maya Ballgame." *Il sacro e il paesaggio nell' America indigena* (2003): 197–198. Web. 21 May 2014.

3. Jared Diamond. *Collapse*. New York: Viking, 2005. Print. 157–158.

4. Ibid.

5. Sandra Blakeslee. "Linguists Solve Riddles of Ancient Maya Language." *New York Times*. New York Times, 4 Apr. 1989. Web. 21 May 2014.

6. Simon Martin. *Chronicle of the Maya Kings and Queens*. New York: Thames, 2000. Print. 28.

Chapter 2. From Simple Farmers to City Builders

1. "Paleoindian." *Illinois State Museum*. Illinois State Museum, 2000. Web. 15 May 2014.

2. Larry Peterson and Gerald H. Haug. "Climate and the Collapse of Maya Civilization: A Series of Multi-year Droughts Helped Doom an Ancient Culture." *American Scientist* 93.4 (2005): 324. Print.

3. Ibid. 322.

Chapter 3. City-States

1. Heather McKillop. *The Ancient Maya: New Perspectives*. New York: Norton, 2004. Print. 251.

Chapter 4. Maya Society

1. Ramon Carrasco Vargas, Veronica A. Vazquez Lopez, and Simon Martin. "Daily Life of the Ancient Maya Recorded on Murals at Calakmul, Mexico." *Proceedings of the National Academy of Science* 106.46 (17 Nov. 2009): 19248. Print.

2. Lisa J. LeCount and Jason Yaeger. "Provincial Politics and Current Models of the Maya State." *Classic Maya Provincial Politics: Xunantunich and Its Hinterlands*. Eds. Lisa J. LeCount and Jason Yaeger. Tucson, AZ: U of Arizona P, 2010. Print. 24.

Chapter 5. Written Wonders

1. "Cracking the Maya Code." *NOVA*. PBS, 9 Apr. 2008. Web. 2 Oct. 2014.

2. Ibid.

3. Simon Martin. *Chronicle of the Maya Kings and Queens*. New York: Thames, 2000. Print. 11.

4. Alessandro Pezzati. "The Excavation of the Hieroglyphic Stairway at Copan." *Expedition* Spring 2012: 4. Print.

5. "Cracking the Maya Code." *NOVA*. PBS, 9 Apr. 2008. Web. 2 Oct. 2014.

6. Ibid.

SOURCE NOTES CONTINUED

Chapter 6. Gods and Sacrifices

None.

Chapter 7. Mathematical Marvels

1. Julia Miller. "The Caracol, or Observatory, of Chichén Itza." *Yucatan Today*. Yucatan Today, 2008. Web. 15 May 2014.

Chapter 8. At War

1. Zach Zorich. "Defending a Jungle Kingdom." *Archaeology* 64.5 (Sept./Oct. 2011): 38. Print.

Chapter 9. Here and Gone

1. Joseph Stromberg. "Why Did Mayan Civilization Collapse? A New Study Points to Deforestation and Climate Change." *Smithsonian.com*. Smithsonian, 13 Aug. 2012. Web. 19 May 2014.

2. Ibid.

3. Larry Peterson and Gerald H. Haug. "Climate and the Collapse of Maya Civilization: A Series of Multi-year Droughts Helped Doom an Ancient Culture." *American Scientist* 93.4 (2005): 324. Print.

4. "Tikal National Park." *World Heritage Convention*. UNESCO, 2014. Web. 1 May 2014.

5. Michael E. Smith. "The Role of Ancient Cities in Research on Contemporary Urbanization." *UGEC Viewpoints* 8 (Nov. 2012): 15. Print.

6. Angela M. H. Schuster. "Rituals of the Modern Maya." *Archaeology* 50.4 (July/Aug. 1997). Web. 22 May 2014.

7. Ibid.

INDEX

ABOUT THE AUTHOR

Sue Bradford Edwards writes nonfiction for children and teens, working from her home in Saint Louis, Missouri. She studied archaeology and history in college and worked as an archaeological illustrator, drawing funeral medallions buried in a historic cemetery in Saint Louis. Her writing for young readers covers a wide range of topics, including science, horses, and history.